D0017356

I Am
Sacagawea

By Grace Norwich

Illustrated by
Anthony VanArsdale

Received On:

MAY 08 2013

SCHOLASTIC INC. Fremont Library

If you purchased this book without a cover, you should be aware that this book is stolen property. It was reported as "unsold and destroyed" to the publisher, and neither the author nor the publisher has received any payment for this "stripped book."

No part of this publication may be reproduced, stored in a retrieval system, or transmitted in any form or by any means, electronic, mechanical, photocopying, recording, or otherwise, without written permission of the publisher. For information regarding permission, write to Scholastic Inc., Attention: Permissions Department, 557 Broadway, New York, NY 10012.

Copyright © 2012 by Scholastic Inc.

All rights reserved. Published by Scholastic Inc. SCHOLASTIC and associated logos are trademarks and/or registered trademarks of Scholastic Inc.

ISBN 978-0-545-40574-4

10 9 8 7 6 5 4 3 2 1   12 13 14 15 16 17/0

Printed in the U.S.A.   40
First printing, August 2012

Cover illustration by Mark Fredrickson
Interior illustrations by Anthony VanArsdale
Book design by Kay Petronio

Contents

Introduction

Did you ever think you couldn't do something because of who you are or where you come from? Well, my story is proof that anything is possible.

In the early days of the United States of America, life was hard for a lot of people. Pioneers faced harsh weather, lack of food, and wild animals. But life was especially hard for me. Born an Indian girl, I didn't have many rights or much freedom. The white people trading and traveling the land were either scared of Indians or thought we were inferior. Even within my tribe, women were treated as property to be traded just like horses.

No one imagined that I was destined for more than cooking, cleaning, gathering food, raising children, and obeying my husband. Yet, while I was still a teen, I not only accompanied the explorers Captain Meriwether Lewis and Lieutenant William Clark on one of the most important trips ever made on this continent, I also ensured that the voyage was a success.

Our 4,000-mile journey west from the center of the country to the Pacific Ocean was filled with all kinds of danger. We braved rough rivers, near starvation, illnesses, rugged mountains, and terrifying storms. Our goal was to map the unknown area and find a route to the sea for future generations. And I did it with a newborn baby strapped to my back.

Brought along to translate for the Indians we would meet along the way, I demonstrated courage, kindness, and competence in all that

I did. Whether pointing out the best way to travel over mountains or finding roots for the men to eat, I did my best to help the group.

Of course, the mission's success wasn't mine alone. It was due to people from different cultures and places trusting one another and working together. I did go on to become one of the most famous Indians and women in history. However, my biggest triumph was personal. Seeing the great Pacific Ocean, I knew I had achieved more than I, or anyone else, could ever have imagined. I am Sacagawea.

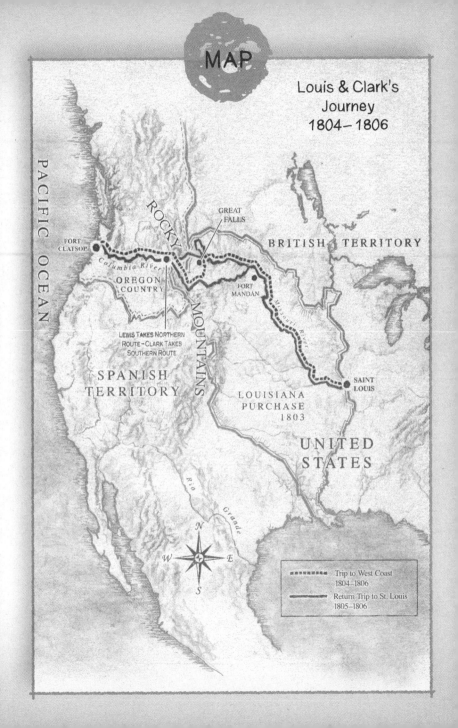

People You Will Meet

SACAGAWEA:
The teenage member of the Shoshone tribe who helped guide and translate during Lewis and Clark's expedition to the Pacific Ocean. She became a national hero.

JUMPING FISH:
Sacagawea's childhood friend, who was also kidnapped by members of the Hidatsa tribe. Jumping Fish, known for her quick moves, escaped and made it back to her tribe.

TOUSSAINT CHARBONNEAU:
The French–Canadian fur trader who was living among the Hidatsa when he married Sacagawea and used his young wife to negotiate a well–paid spot on Lewis and Clark's expedition.

JEAN–BAPTISTE CHARBONNEAU:
The son of Sacagawea and Charbonneau. The infant was not even two months old when he was strapped to his mother's back to cross the continent.

MERIWETHER LEWIS:
President Thomas Jefferson's personal secretary, who headed up the Corps of Discovery to find a route from St. Louis to the Pacific Ocean.

WILLIAM CLARK:
The military officer who was asked by his friend Lewis to be cocaptain of the Corps of Discovery. He developed a special friendship with Sacagawea and eventually wanted to adopt Jean–Baptiste.

CAMEAHWAIT:
Sacagawea's brother and the chief of her Shoshone band. He traded the horses that allowed the Corps of Discovery to make it over the Rockies and on to their final destination.

Time Line

1788 or 1789

Sacagawea is born into the Shoshone tribe in the present-day area of Salmon River, Idaho.

1800

Sacagawea is kidnapped by members of the Hidatsa tribe.

1803

President Thomas Jefferson completes the Louisiana Purchase from France and asks Captain Meriwether Lewis and Lieutenant William Clark to explore the large, unknown territory and find a trail to the Pacific Ocean. They call the expedition the Corps of Discovery.

April 1805

The Corps of Discovery leaves Fort Mandan, Sacagawea with her two-month-old infant strapped to her back.

June 1805

Sacagawea nearly dies of a fever, but Clark nurses her back to health.

June 29, 1805

Sacagawea almost drowns, along with Clark, Charbonneau, and baby Jean-Baptiste, in a flash flood near the Great Falls.

January 1806

Sacagawea makes it to the Pacific Ocean.

March 23, 1806

The Corps of Discovery turns around to head home.

August 14, 1806

The corps arrives back at Fort Mandan. Clark offers to adopt Jean-Baptiste, but Sacagawea, Charbonneau, and their baby remain in the village.

November 1804

Lewis and Clark arrive near the villages of the Mandan, where Sacagawea is living with her husband, Toussaint Charbonneau. The explorers agree that the Indian teenager will accompany them on their journey to translate and negotiate with other Indians they meet on the voyage.

February 11, 1805

Sacagawea gives birth to a baby boy, whom she names Jean–Baptiste.

August 1805

When the Corps of Discovery arrives in Shoshone territory, Sacagawea is reunited with her tribe and with her brother Cameahwait, who is now the chief.

August 30, 1805

After Sacagawea helps the Corps of Discovery trade with the Shoshone for horses, she says good–bye to her tribe as the explorers head into the Rocky Mountains.

December 20, 1812

Sacagawea dies of a fever at Fort Manuel in present–day South Dakota, according to the diary of John Luttig, a clerk.

April 9, 1884

An Indian woman who is about ninety–four years old dies. Indians and missionaries living on the reservation are sure she is Sacagawea.

CHAPTER ONE

A Childhood in the Wild

The native peoples, who lived in North America long before the United States existed, had a diverse group of cultures, despite the fact that the white settlers who arrived called all of them Indians. (The name actually comes from the explorer Christopher Columbus, who thought he had landed in the Indies when he arrived in America and called its inhabitants Indians.)

Just like people from different countries, members of different Indian tribes spoke

completely different languages and had different **customs**—even when they lived right near
one another! Some tribes were wealthier, others
poorer. Some farmed the land, while others
existed by fishing, hunting, and gathering.
When members of two tribes who didn't speak
the same language wanted to communicate,
they used sign language or pictures drawn on
the ground with a stick.

Often when different tribes came in contact with one another, it was in battle. Indians fought regularly, attacking villages or camps in search of guns, horses, food, and people. Whoever proved to be the fiercest warriors took women and children as prisoners back to their own camp.

The Shoshone—the large tribe into which Sacagawea was born in 1788 or 1789—had groups called bands all over present-day Utah, Wyoming, Idaho, and Nevada. *Shoshone* means "snake" and was a name that other Indians called the tribe because they associated them with the Snake River. But the tribe called themselves *Nermenuh*, or "people."

Sacagawea's band, called the Lemhi Shoshone,

lived so deep in the wilderness they didn't have any contact with white people until Lewis and Clark arrived. During the long, bitterly cold winters, they stayed in their village located in the Rocky Mountains. Wrapped in rabbit skins to keep warm, the men hunted for deer or mountain sheep. They were also known for raising powerful horses that could travel over

the rocky **terrain**. Women worked just as hard, caring for children, drying meat, preparing furs and skins, cooking meals, and searching for berries and edible plants. Whether meat or roots, food was often scarce.

Spending most of the year in the harsh Rocky Mountains wasn't exactly their choice. The Lemhi often warred with the Hidatsa tribe that had control of the land near the intersection of the Missouri and Knife rivers, which was **fertile** from all the water rushing through it. The Hidatsa, who grew corn, squash, and tobacco, traded crops with other Indians for horses, hides, and blankets.

Then they would trade these goods with the white men coming down the rivers in exchange for guns and ammunition. The

guns made the Hidatsa practically invincible. The Lemhi, who only had bows and arrows to protect themselves, were forced to retreat into the cold mountains.

In the summer, however, Sacagawea's band would have to come down from the mountains in search of buffalo. They used every part of the animal: the meat for food, the skins for clothing, the bones for needles and dishes, the **tendons** for **tepees**, and the **sinew** for thread. The threat of the Hidatsa was always there, but finding a buffalo was essential to the Lemhis' survival.

The summer Sacagawea was about twelve years old, her band was on the way to their regular summer camp in Three Forks, Montana, named for the three rivers that meet at one point. The area was perfect for hunting, with cool mountain breezes coming off the Rockies and plenty of wildlife. The abundance of water meant lots of berries and plants for the women to gather.

It was a day like any other. Sacagawea left her parents, brother, and sister to join her friend Jumping Fish (who got her name because she was always darting around quickly like a fish in water). As she plucked the berries growing alongside a sparkling stream, perhaps Sacagawea was daydreaming about her future. As a young girl, her father had promised her as a wife to a much older man. Women and girls in her tribe were considered the property of their fathers and husbands. Soon enough she would have to go live with the man and everything about her life would change.

Whether or not Sacagawea was daydreaming, she didn't hear the Hidatsa warriors creeping up behind her on horseback. The women and children, busy with their tasks, had no clue they were silently surrounded. That is, until Lemhi men spotted their enemies and tried to attack. The awful sounds of men and horses fighting filled what had been a peaceful scene only seconds before.

The Shoshone launched arrows at the Hidatsa on their thrashing horses. But the Hidatsa returned with gunfire that brought down the Shoshone men. The loud crack of the guns and the swift destruction terrified the Shoshone men, who turned their horses around and galloped away.

A few women and children ran after the men from their tribe, but they couldn't keep up with the horses. Their eyes stung from the dust

cloud left by the retreating Shoshone. Within seconds the Hidatsa were upon them.

Meanwhile, Sacagawea rushed into the river. She scrambled through the icy rushing waters, aiming for one of the small islands where she could hide in the tall grass. Then one of the Hidatsa men grabbed her and lifted her onto his horse. Sacagawea had been captured!

What Does *Sacagawea* Mean, Anyway?

Like most Indian tribes, the Lemhi Shoshone had an oral–history culture. That means that history (including Sacagawea's name) was passed down by people saying it out loud rather than writing it down. When people did eventually write her name down in stories, they spelled it many different ways, including "Sacajawea," "Sacagawea," and "Sakakawea." (Lewis and Clark, who were very bad spellers, had fourteen different spellings of her name in their journals!) Depending on how it's pronounced, her name means "boat pusher" or "bird woman." Many scholars think "bird woman" makes more sense; why would people who live in the mountains name a baby "boat pusher"?

The warrior held her tightly in his arms while he rode back to his village. As she left behind everything and everyone she knew, Sacagawea may have wondered what was going to happen.

New Worlds to Explore

In some ways, life in the Hidatsa village wasn't all that different from life in Sacagawea's home. She had to work very hard preparing hides, drying meat, sewing, and doing everything else Indian women were expected to do. However, that's where the comparisons ended. In the cluster of villages on the Missouri River near present-day Bismarck, North Dakota, over six thousand Hidatsa and Mandan lived together. Unlike her tribe, which used tepees

for shelter as they moved around in search of food, the Hidatsa farmed the land and lived in solid earthen huts. They also spoke a completely different language. When she first arrived, Sacagawea had no one to talk to since her friend Jumping Fish, who had also been captured, managed to escape and find a way back to the Lemhi. The young Indian girl must have been very lonely.

Sacagawea learned to speak the Hidatsa language, and after three years with the tribe was considered old enough to be married. She had no choice in the matter. Sacagawea was sold to Toussaint Charbonneau, a French-Canadian fur trader who was known to have a bad temper. At least twenty years older than Sacagawea, Charbonneau had been living among the Hidatsa and Mandan for some time before they were married. Charbonneau became friendly with his Indian neighbors, learned to speak their language, and adopted many of their customs. One of the customs he adopted was the common practice for men to have more than one wife. When Charbonneau married Sacagawea, he already had another wife, named Otter Woman.

While Sacagawea was adapting to a whole new way of life, thousands of miles away the president of the United States, in Washington, D.C., bought land from France that doubled the size of the country. In 1803, Thomas Jefferson paid the French government about $15 million for the Louisiana Purchase. That bought 828,000 square miles of land, which included the present-day states of North Dakota, South Dakota, Nebraska, Oklahoma,

Thomas Jefferson

The Louisiana Purchase

Emperor Napoleon Bonaparte had a dream of creating an empire in the New World for France. To do this, he wanted the 828,000–square–mile territory of Louisiana, which was controlled at that time by Spain. Although he made a deal with Spain for the land, wars in other parts of the world kept French troops from reaching Louisiana and being able to defend it. As soon as President Jefferson heard about the transfer of the territory from Spain to France, he approached Napoleon about buying the area around New Orleans. Jefferson wanted to be able to sail vessels down the Mississippi River, and there were already many American settlers living in the area. At first Napoleon refused, but then he had a change of heart. A big one. He offered the United States not only New Orleans but all of Louisiana!

Arkansas, and Missouri, as well as parts of seven more states. At the time, however, the region was almost completely unexplored and unknown.

Jefferson, the third president of the United States, needed someone to travel this mysterious land and bring back information. He wanted to know all about the geography, the plants, the animals, and the people of the area. But even more important, he wanted to find a trail from St. Louis, Missouri, to the Pacific Ocean. At that time, St. Louis was the last point of civilization before the wild, western frontier began. Jefferson hoped the Missouri River, just a few miles north, would be the start of a new trade route.

Jefferson asked his twenty-nine-year-old personal secretary, Meriwether Lewis, to organize an expedition to investigate the new land. It became known as the Corps of

Meriwether Lewis

William Clark

Northwest Passage

During their expedition, Jefferson hoped that Lewis and Clark would find the Northwest Passage. This was a waterway that, legend had it, traveled from the Atlantic Ocean all the way to the Pacific. No one knew if it really existed, but if it did, trading would be much easier. Goods could travel by boat instead of wagons trudging over mountains and through plains. The Northwest Passage would be discovered, but not until a hundred years later. The Norwegian explorer Roald Amundsen found a direct passage from one side of the continent to the other during a sailing expedition in 1903. Unfortunately, the route, which is five hundred miles north of the Arctic Circle, took three years to travel because of giant icebergs and treacherous seas.

Discovery. The president told Lewis, "The object of your mission is to explore the Missouri River, & such principal stream of it [. . . to find out what] may offer the most direct & practicable water communication across this continent for the purposes of commerce."

That was a straightforward request. The journey, however, would be anything but straightforward. Lewis had no idea what he would find when he stepped into the wilderness. He needed help to lead this trip. So he called on his good friend William Clark, a thirty-three-year-old military officer. Both had

been in the army and had a lot of experience living out in the wild. They could hunt and fish, make shelters, and defend themselves against enemies.

After finding about forty soldiers, hunters, and boatmen to join their adventure (including Clark's slave York), the corps set off for St. Louis, where they spent the winter of 1803. Lewis insisted on bringing along his dog, Seaman, a Newfoundland who could swim better than the men, most of whom couldn't swim at all. There they waited out the harsh winter weather. Then in May 1804, after the ice had thawed, they set off on the Missouri River, not sure who or what they would find.

CHAPTER THREE

The Newest (and Littlest) Member of the Corps

When the Corps of Discovery arrived at the Hidatsa and Mandan villages in the fall of 1804, it was big news. Unlike Sacagawea's band of the Lemhi, who had never seen white people before, these tribes were used to foreigners coming through the area to trade. Still, word spread quickly from hut to hut about the men in the boats. They didn't have a lot of entertainment, and this definitely counted as such.

The weather had already turned, so Lewis and Clark set up camp for the winter across the river from the villages. They couldn't travel during the coldest months (the temperature could drop to 50 degrees below freezing), and it was as good a place as any to wait for spring.

The Indians they met seemed friendly, but Lewis and Clark wanted them to stay that way. So they invited the Indian chiefs over many times to give them gifts, such as shiny medals bearing the image of Thomas Jefferson. They also explained that the corps came in peace. The Indians approved and returned with gifts of corn and other crops they had grown, as well as buffalo meat. Everyone was happy with the exchange.

With winter approaching, the corps got busy building a shelter. Fort Mandan consisted of eight cabins made from cottonwood trees,

the cracks stuffed with rags and grass for insulation. They also built a high stockade with a gate and lock, just in case the Indians decided to stop being friendly.

Charbonneau, like any smart trader, was always trying to figure out if he possessed anything with which he could make a profit.

Opportunities like the Corps of Discovery didn't pass through the villages every day. Everyone knew the travelers were headed to the sea, and  to reach the sea they would have to pass over the Rockies. They would never make it through the mountains without horses. However, they couldn't get horses from the Hidatsa and Mandan villages because they still needed to travel a good distance by water before arriving at the mountain range. That meant the corps would have to trade for horses with the Shoshone when they got to the Rockies.

A light went off in Charbonneau's head. He was in the ideal position for a trader because he had something the corps needed desperately: Sacagawea.

As a member of the Shoshone tribe, she would easily be able to negotiate for horses. Plus she spoke both Shoshone and Hidatsa fluently, so she could act as a translator. Charbonneau headed over to Fort Mandan to make a deal.

The fur trader was right. Lewis and Clark wanted Sacagawea to join the expedition. She would translate Shoshone into Hidatsa for Charbonneau, who would translate it into French for corps member Francois Labiche, who would then translate it into English. One conversation could take forever, but at least the captains would be able to understand the Indians. They offered Charbonneau $25 a month, three to five times what the other members of the corps were making. Lewis and Clark were very glad to have Sacagawea on board, although they weren't quite as excited about Charbonneau. Lewis wrote, "[He] was useful as an interpreter only."

A week after the men sealed the deal with a handshake, Sacagawea arrived at Fort Mandan with Charbonneau. They planned to live with the rest of the corps until it was time to continue the expedition. Lewis and Clark met the teenage Indian, who presented them with a beautiful hand-sewn buffalo robe.

After she gave them the heavy garment, they learned something they hadn't known about Sacagawea before: She was seven months pregnant!

The Journals of the Corps of Discovery

Lewis and Clark were expected to keep detailed journals as part of the mission for the president. They documented their travels through writing and drawings. Almost everything scholars know about the expedition comes from their journals. What Lewis, Clark, and other men on the expedition wrote totals nearly five thousand pages! Although Lewis and Clark mention Sacagawea some three dozen times, none of the entries mention her actual words and very few talk about how she felt.

To see the text of the actual journals (yes, all five thousand pages), check out lewisandclarkjournals.unl.edu.

Lewis and Clark would share many adventures with Sacagawea, but the first one was when she gave birth. She went into labor on February 11, 1805, in Fort Mandan, which was filled with men who didn't have a clue how to deliver a baby. Neither did Sacagawea, since this was her first child. Lewis, who tended to her, wrote in his journal that "her labor was tedious and the pain violent."

While Sacagawea struggled with contractions, someone at the fort told Lewis to give her the rattle of a rattlesnake to eat. In an extraordinary stroke of luck, Lewis had some rattles in the samples of plant and animal life he had been collecting to bring back to the president. Ten minutes after eating the rattle,

Sacagawea gave birth to a baby boy named Jean-Baptiste. He became the littlest member of the corps.

CHAPTER FOUR

The Journey Begins!

On Sunday, April 7, 1805, the Corps of Discovery was finally ready to set off on their journey. Sacagawea wrapped up her baby, whom the men called Little Baptiste, and strapped him to her back in a cradleboard, which is a piece of wood with leather laces. Baptiste was snug and secure as Sacagawea said good-bye to Otter Woman, Charbonneau's other wife, and other friends she had made in the last five years. Then she got into one of the boats filled with a total of thirty-two people, equipment for the expedition, and Seaman, the dog.

The Hidatsa and Mandan villages slowly receded into the distance as the boats headed up the Missouri River. Lewis was filled with both hope and fear as they paddled toward the unknown. He had no idea what was going to happen, but he wasn't nervous at all. "Entertaining as I do, the most confident hope of succeeding in a voyage," he wrote, "I could but esteem this moment of my departure as among the most happy of my life."

The expedition was difficult from the start. Traveling west on the Missouri River, the corps was going against the current. The paddling

Equipment
Check

 Two pirogues (open boats hollowed from a log with sails and flat bottoms that made them easier for fishing and shallow rivers)

 Several canoes made from cottonwood trees

Tepee materials: dried buffalo skins to tie around a dozen wooden poles

Guns and ammunition

Mapping instruments

Medicine

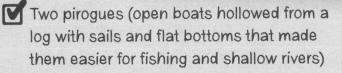

 Fourteen bales of presents for the Indians, including red, white, and blue beads (blue was the Indians' favorite kind)

 Journals for writing

Yards of oilcloth to wrap the goods and keep out dampness and mold

was exhausting and sometimes got so tough
that the men had to get out and push the boats.
Even though it was spring, the river was still
ice-cold. As they pushed, the men's feet and
legs would be freezing as well as banged up
from rocks and sunken logs.

Sacagawea might not have pushed the boats, but the young woman quickly proved she was as capable and willing to help as anyone else on the expedition. And she was the only one who also had to tend to a newborn!  She was especially good at gathering wild food, something the rest of the corps didn't know anything about. Digging in the ground, she unearthed wild artichokes, licorice, and a root they called white apple. The men hungrily gobbled up whatever she found since they needed all the nourishment they could get.

Sacagawea wasn't just skilled at finding food. About a month after they left the Indian villages, they were traveling on the river when a sudden gust of wind hit the boat. The wind

was so strong it pushed the boat on its side and water began to rush in. Charbonneau panicked. Like most of the other men in the boat, who were also very frightened, he couldn't swim. Charbonneau ("the most timid waterman in the world," as Lewis described him) grabbed the sides of the boat and started screaming and praying. Meanwhile, the boat, which also carried Sacagawea and her baby, was filling

Pirogue

with more water and threatening to completely capsize.

Lewis and Clark, who had been walking on the shore alongside the boats, fired their guns to get the men's attention, calm them down, and give orders. As Charbonneau wailed, they were terrified that all the medicine and other

goods on board were going to wind up floating down the river.

A few of the men began paddling to shore while others bailed water out of the boat to keep it from sinking. The captains breathed a sigh of relief and then noticed something remarkable. Among the hysteria, there was Sacagawea calmly holding Baptiste in one hand and retrieving goods that had washed overboard with the other. If she was scared, she didn't show it. Because she maintained a level head, the corps only lost a few items.

Lewis and Clark recognized that Sacagawea was a special woman, both courageous and capable. In his journal, Lewis described her as having "equal fortitude and resolution, with any person onboard at the time of the accedent." The captains were so impressed that a few days later they named a branch of the river after Sacagawea.

CHAPTER FIVE

Danger Ahead

The boat accident was just the start of the trouble. Sacagawea was about to face death—and this time she would have to rely on others to help her.

In early June, Sacagawea came down with a terrible fever. Because they didn't have antibiotics yet, when someone had an infection there was nothing to do but wait it out and hope for the best. Sacagawea was likely suffering from an infection as her fever rose

higher and higher.

Clark, who saw how much she was suffering, took care of her. He sat with Sacagawea through the night, applying bark poultices (soft materials applied to the body to relieve soreness or inflammation). He hoped they would make her better, but her condition only worsened.

The corps had been waiting for Sacagawea to get better before they moved on, but they couldn't wait any longer. They had to push on if they were going to make it across the Rockies before camping for winter. Every day counted. So Clark laid Sacagawea down in a shaded spot in the pirogue. He administered two kinds of painkillers he had on the trip. But she continued to suffer, especially since she was in an uncomfortable boat, holding on to her baby, who was still breast-feeding.

It seemed like a miracle, but a week after she came down with the fever, Sacagawea showed small signs of improving. Her recovery

was slow, but eventually she started walking and sipping buffalo broth.

Nobody was more relieved than Clark. During her illness, he and Sacagawea developed a special friendship. It became clear that he thought of her as a person, not an inferior. He also cared about Baptiste, whom he described as beautiful and intelligent. After Sacagawea had completely recovered, she usually walked with Clark along the shore rather than riding in the pirogue.

Any sense of ease they had didn't last for long. Soon after Sacagawea got better, the Corps of Discovery came upon the Great Falls of the Missouri River. The series of five waterfalls dropped the river a total of 612 feet. It was an amazing sight, "the grandest sight I ever beheld," Lewis wrote. The sun mixed with the mist from the falls to create beautiful rainbows.

The falls were impressive, but they were also a real problem. There was no way the corps could get their boats over them. The only option was to carry all their equipment and boats overland. Without any pack animals like horses or mules to help, it took over a month of

The Great Falls Today

Today, only one of the Great Falls exists in its natural state. The rest of them were dammed starting in the late 1800s.

backbreaking pushing, pulling, and heaving to get their gear around the falls.

One day while they were making their way around the falls, Clark, Sacagawea, Baptiste, and Charbonneau were walking

along the riverbank when the weather suddenly turned stormy. The sky went steel gray and the wind whipped hard. A bad storm was brewing.

Clark told everyone to move into a dry **gully** below them to take shelter under some overhanging rocks. They scrambled down as beating rain mixed with hail fell from the sky. Looking down at their feet, they realized the gully was filling with water. Clark, who normally dispensed good, sound advice, had led everyone into danger! A tidal wave of muddy, rocky water raged down the ravine carrying boulders, tree trunks, and anything else it could pull with it. The water was now up to their waists and getting stronger by the second. It was pushing them toward an 87-foot waterfall only a quarter mile away. Charbonneau froze with fear.

Clark had gotten them into this mess, and

he had to get them out. First he shoved
Charbonneau up the gully. Then he pushed
Sacagawea with Baptiste up the slippery

mud and rocks. Charbonneau pulled them up the rest of the way, and Clark quickly followed behind, making it over the end just before a flash flood filled the gully with raging water.

CHAPTER SIX

Home Again

Sacagawea was walking behind Lewis. Baptiste was snug and sleeping in his cradleboard as usual. Passing a stream bending around a pile of rocks, she had a funny feeling. The brush, the little islands in the water, where had she seen them before? Suddenly it came to her: This was the place where she had been kidnapped!

The corps had arrived at Three Forks, the buffalo hunting grounds of the Shoshone, and the site where Sacagawea had been carried off by the Hidatsa years ago. She told the captains what had happened in this spot, and they grew excited. They must be near the Shoshone. They were eager to find Sacagawea's tribe because they needed to trade for horses to cross the Rockies.

Despite his eagerness to locate members of the tribe, Clark could not go on. A painful **boil** on one of his ankles made it impossible for him to walk. As with Sacagawea's fever, the expedition could not delay for illness or injury. So Lewis set off with three men on foot, while Clark followed slowly by canoe with the others.

It didn't take long for Lewis to find a few Shoshone. Women and children collecting food either took off running or fell to the ground when they saw the men approach. They were terrified and thought they were going to be killed or kidnapped. This was a crucial moment. If one of the women ran back to her camp and reported that there were hostile men in the area, they could be attacked. If they jeopardized their chances for getting those

horses in any way, the entire expedition would be ruined.

Lewis slowly reached into his pocket. The Shoshone cowered, but he didn't take out a gun or a knife. Instead he pulled out a little pot of red paint and gently applied it to the cheeks of the women. The paint was actually red earth that Sacagawea had pointed out to Lewis and Clark. She explained that the Shoshone used the earth as face paint in a symbol of peace. Lewis, who had collected the earth in a small bottle, also gave the women gifts of beads, awls (small tools for punching holes), and **pewter** mirrors.

The message came through loud and clear, and the women led Lewis and his men back to their camp. But as

the men followed happily, they heard a loud rumble, as if a huge thunderstorm was brewing. They turned just as sixty Shoshone warriors on their horses

surrounded them. Facing the men, Lewis slowly held up a small U.S. flag as another sign of peace. The Indians hopped off their horses and got very close to Lewis and his team, who shivered with fear. Then the Indians raised their arms and gave the white men big . . . hugs!

Lewis was taken immediately to the chief, whose name was Cameahwait, meaning "one who never walks." It was a good thing Lewis had studied his Indian customs so thoroughly.

As everyone sat in a circle, he took off his moccasins. Lewis's action was an important Shoshone ritual that symbolized sincerity—if a person did not keep the promises he made during the council, the gesture said, he would go barefoot for the rest of his life.

Cameahwait's Headdress

The Shoshone appreciated the gesture, but Lewis knew that if he was going to trade for the desperately needed horses, he needed Sacagawea. Through sign language and drawing, he asked Cameahwait and some of the tribe members to come back with him to the river fork where the rest of the corps would be waiting. The chief wasn't confident about the idea. He didn't know Lewis and his men. They could easily be setting up an ambush. But Lewis convinced them that no harm would come to them.

When they arrived at the meeting spot, nobody was there. Not Sacagawea. Not Clark. Not a soul. The situation grew tense. Cameahwait was suspicious. This had all the makings of a trap. Lewis felt the silent pressure rising. If the Shoshone didn't trust him, they would either kill them or simply take off—riding away with their last chance for horses

and essentially ending the expedition. He had to do something. Lewis slowly went for his gun. The Indians instantly raised their bows and arrows. But Lewis put up his other hand in a signal to stop. He took the gun out slowly and handed it to Cameahwait. Everyone—

whites and Indians—was shocked. Then Lewis had the three corps members do the same. This was the ultimate sign of trust.

It took until the next morning (nobody slept during the night) for a few small figures to appear bobbing on the river in the distance. When the two groups were close enough to see each other, Sacagawea, who had been walking on the shore alongside the boats, was overcome with joy. She recognized the Indians, and they recognized her. The corps hadn't just found the Shoshone, they had found Sacagawea's band, the Lemhi!

It seemed like a miracle. Reunited with the very people who had raised her, Sacagawea danced to show how happy she was.

Back at the Lemhi camp, Jumping Fish ran out of the crowd and rushed into Sacagawea's arms. The two old friends who had been kidnapped together embraced each other as if each couldn't believe the other woman was real. No one else could understand what they had been through; they had so much to tell each other.

Sacagawea couldn't catch up for long, because she had a job to do. The chief, Lewis, and Clark were already in the tent making formal introductions. She opened up the flaps of the tent and silently took a seat with her head bowed. When she lifted up her gaze, she saw something even more incredible than Jumping Fish: Her brother was the chief!

There were plenty of tears and hugging. Sadly, this was the only family reunion for

Travois

A horse travois was used to drag heavy loads.

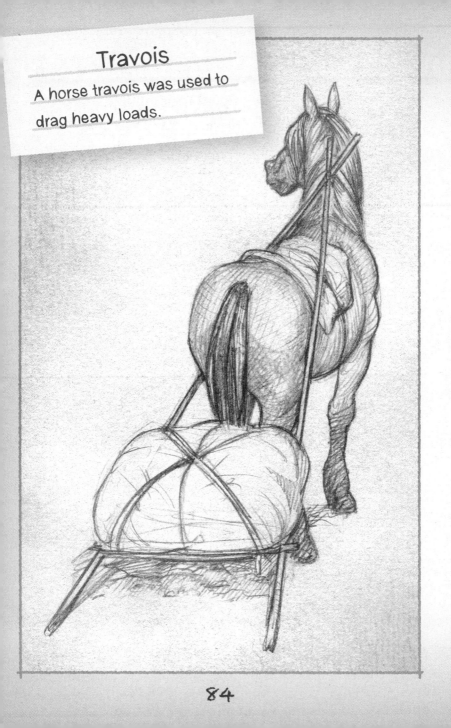

Sacagawea. She soon learned from her brother that her parents and her sister were dead. It was hard for her to interpret with all the emotions she felt. "Her new situation seemed to overpower her, and she was frequently interrupted by her tears," Clark wrote. Through the tears and three languages, Sacagawea related the main point of their visit: Lewis and Clark needed horses for the next part of their expedition crossing the Rockies. The chief wanted guns so they could put up more of a fight against the Hidatsa. They made a deal: twenty-nine horses in exchange for pistols, gunpowder, and knives.

The corps stayed with the Lemhi as the captains consulted with Cameahwait about the way to the ocean. Clark, still holding out hope of finding the Northwest Passage, went on a mini-expedition on the rough rapids of the Lemhi and Salmon rivers, where he quickly realized the chief was right: The only way to travel was over the mountains. Too soon the day came for Sacagawea to say good-bye to her friends and family.

Sacagawea didn't stay with the Lemhi people. She had been raised in the band, but it was no longer her life. She had a husband whom she belonged to and a baby she needed to take care of. Plus, she needed to accompany Lewis and Clark on the last leg of their journey. Sacagawea knew this part of the country better than anyone else in the corps. She had a job to do.

CHAPTER SEVEN

The Journey Is a Success!

The trek over the Rocky Mountains was harder than any of them could have ever imagined. At some points the incline was so steep that even the sure-footed horses started to slip. The men would have to take the heavy loads off the horses and carry the supplies themselves until the ground leveled off again.

It was not yet winter. Still, snow came up to their knees as they got higher, and sleet froze the rest of their bodies. On top of all this, food

was running dangerously low. There were no berries to gather or deer to be hunted.

They met up with a small group of Indians who kindly gave them some of their food and traded a few tired horses for new ones, but they couldn't rest long. They needed to push ahead in order to make their goal of reaching the Pacific before real winter set in.

The corps, weak and freezing, was miserable. "I have been wet and as cold in every part as I ever was in my life, indeed I was at one time fearfull my feet would freeze in the thin mockersons which I wore," Clark wrote.

When they stumbled out onto the Weippe Prairie, they were exhausted and starving, but alive. The friendly Nez Perce tribe greeted them with food that the corps gratefully feasted on. The dried fish and berries the Indians offered were so delicious the men gorged on them until they became sick.

A Friendly Face

Wherever the Corps of Discovery traveled, they met different tribes of Indians. No matter the band, Sacagawea proved invaluable. She "reconciles all the Indians, as to our friendly intentions. a woman with a party of men is a token of peace," Clark explained.

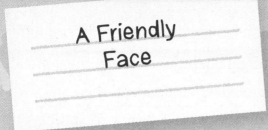

After the travelers regained their strength, the Indians gave them good news: The Pacific was only twelve days away. But there was also bad news. The three rivers they had to travel to get there had some fierce and dangerous rapids. A couple of Nez Perce Indians went with the corps to help them navigate the rough water of the Clearwater River. On October 16, nine days after leaving the prairie, they made it to the Columbia

River, which would take them directly to the ocean!

Their destination was so close but so far away. By early November, they were only about 20 miles from the ocean, but they had to stop and make camp. The river was rocking with waves, making everyone, including Sacagawea, very seasick. With winter almost upon them, they stopped to build a camp on the Pacific Coast. They named the camp Fort Clatsop in honor of the Indians who lived in the area.

It never seemed to stop raining that winter. The corps had to eat rotting meat because there was no way to dry it, and the camp was infested with biting fleas. When Clark fell ill due to the damp weather, Sacagawea had the opportunity to repay him for the way he had nursed her

back to health earlier in their journey.

Not long after New Year's Day in 1806, the corps heard from local Indians that a whale had washed ashore not too far from the camp. Lewis and Clark decided to take a few men

all the way to the shoreline so that they could get meat and blubber to eat. Sacagawea, who wasn't part of the group, spoke up. She hadn't come all this way with a baby on her back not to see the ocean.

It must have been hard for her to speak her mind, but no harder than traveling 4,000 miles in the harsh wild. The trip took five days of treacherous rowing and climbing. And when they arrived at the present-day site of Cannon Beach, Oregon, the whale was nothing but a skeleton picked clean by animals and Indians. Still, Sacagawea reached her goal: to see the great big sea.

CHAPTER EIGHT

Saying Good-bye

On March 23, 1806, the Corps of Discovery turned around to make the long trek home. Going back seemed like it would be easier since they were driven by the satisfaction of achieving their goal and also knew where they were going.

But they had one last big scare. While the group was staying with the Nez Perce again, Baptiste got sick. For eighteen days the little baby who had been over mountains and to the

sea was deathly ill. Lewis and Clark tended to him night and day and wrote about his condition in their journals. Everyone was worried he was going to die. The captains applied onion poultices to his swollen neck until finally the infection cleared. Baptiste survived!

In June the corps headed back into the Rockies. Only this time they had five guides from the Nez Perce who knew the mountains like the backs of their hands. The trip that had taken eleven days the previous fall took only six.

Once they had cleared the Rockies, Lewis and Clark split up to find different routes back to the Mandan villages. Sacagawea went with Clark's group to the Yellowstone River. While on their way to the river, the trail opened onto two different mountain passes. Clark

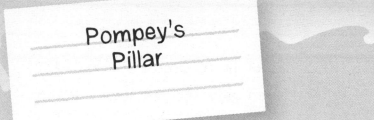

Pompey's Pillar

As they neared the Yellowstone River, Clark and the rest of his group saw a big, flat rock rise up from the plains. On closer inspection, they found carvings from Indians. Inspired, Clark carved his name and the date—July 25, 1806—and named it after Jean–Baptiste, whom he called Pompey. So the rock became Pompey's Pillar.

didn't know which one led to the Yellowstone. But Sacagawea did. This was the land of the Shoshone, where she had been raised.

August 14, 1806—one year and four months after the journey began—the Corps of Discovery arrived back in Fort Mandan. Lewis and Clark never found the water passageway, but they did their job. They mapped the land, found a route, noted the vegetation and geology, and made contact with the Indians. And they never could have done it without Sacagawea, whom Clark said "has been of great service to me as a pilot through this country."

Saying good-bye was almost as hard as making the trip. Clark, who truly came to love Baptiste, wanted to adopt the little boy and give him an education. Charbonneau and Sacagawea declined the kind offer. Their adventure had been amazing, but now it was over.

Sacagawea's Mysterious Death

Three years after the expedition, Sacagawea, Charbonneau, and Jean-Baptiste had a change of heart and decided to join Clark in St. Louis (Charbonneau was motivated by a congressional grant of 320 acres of land). They only stayed for two years before they were back on the road. After Charbonneau sold his land to Clark for $100 and left Baptiste to be educated by the lieutenant, he and Sacagawea joined an expedition to start a fur-trading

post up the Missouri River.

Sacagawea remained in Fort Manuel along the Missouri River in present-day South Dakota, where she gave birth to a daughter named Lisette in August 1812. The fort's clerk, John Luttig, wrote the news of the day in his journal. On Sunday, December 10, he sadly reported that "this Evening the Wife of Charbonau, a Snake Squaw, died Of a putrid fever she was a good and the best Woman in the fort, aged abt 25 years she left a fine infant girl."

From the written evidence, most historians believe Sacagawea returned to South Dakota with Charbonneau in late 1811 and died there a year later.

However, there is a second story that has Sacagawea living to the ripe old age of ninety-four on the Wind River Shoshone reservation in Wyoming. People who claimed to know Sacagawea included teachers, farmers, and even the minister who attended her funeral in 1884.

History is not always cut-and-dry. When you go back into the past, especially far back, it can get confusing. **Scholars** read different accounts from many people to try and figure out what really happened—and what it means.

Though no one can really be sure about Sacagawea's death, everyone can agree that she was a true American hero because she pushed herself beyond the definition others gave her. Sacagawea is the definition of a trailblazer.

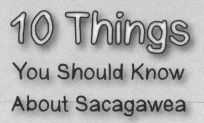

10 Things
You Should Know
About Sacagawea

 Sacagawea was born in 1788 or 1789, in the area now called Salmon, Idaho.

 She was an Indian from the Lemhi band of the Shoshone tribe.

 In 1800, when she was about eleven or twelve, she was kidnapped by the Hidatsa tribe and taken to live in their village.

U.S.
postage
stamp

She married a French—Canadian fur trader, Toussaint Charbonneau, and had a baby boy, named Jean—Baptiste, on February 11, 1805.

In the spring of 1805, Sacagawea and her family joined the Corps of Discovery, the expedition led by Meriwether Lewis and William Clark to find a route from St. Louis to the Pacific Ocean.

Sacagawea not only spoke two Indian languages—Hidatsa and Shoshone—which helped her translate for the corps, she also made encounters with Indian tribes easier because the Indians assumed any group traveling with a woman was peaceful.

When Sacagawea reunited with her band of the Lemhi Shoshone in 1805, she discovered that her brother, Cameahwait, had become chief.

She helped secure horses from the Shoshone, which the corps needed to make it over the Rocky Mountains and complete their journey.

Statue in Bismarck,
North Dakota

 Sacagawea insisted that she join the small group who went all the way to the Pacific Ocean in the beginning of 1806.

 Historians can't agree on when Sacagawea died. It was either at the age of twenty-five or ninety-four.

10 MORE Things
That Are Pretty Cool to Know

 1 Believing they were descended from wolves, the Shoshone tribe considered coyotes and dogs close relatives.

 2 Clark was a big fan of nicknames. He gave the nickname "Janey" to Sacagawea and called Jean—Baptiste "Pompey."

Sucking on fingers, what Sacagawea did when she was reunited with the Lemhi after her kidnapping, was a Shoshone sign for family.

 The Corps of Discovery met nearly fifty different Indian tribes during the expedition.

 Charbonneau was paid $500.33 for the expedition. Sacagawea was paid nothing. (Lewis received a salary of $3,360 for four years of service, while Clark got $2,520.)

Clark measured the length of the expedition from St. Louis to the Pacific Ocean at 4,162 miles—based on modern measurements, Clark was only off by 40 miles!

The debate over Sacagawea's place and date of death got so heated that a private investigator, Charles Eastman, was sent from South Dakota to snoop around Wyoming in 1925. The evidence he found led him to believe she had died on a reservation at ninety-four.

U.S.
golden
dollar coin

When Baptiste was eighteen years old, he met a German prince and traveled back with him to Europe, where he remained for six years. When he returned to the United States, he became a wilderness guide.

There are more monuments to Sacagawea in the United States than to any other woman.

Sacagawea replaced Susan B. Anthony on the $1 coin in January 2000.

Traditional Hidatsa Earthen Hut

Shoshone Tepee

Glossary

Boil: a painful swelling on or under the skin

Custom: a tradition in a culture or society

Fertile: capable of growing many crops or plants

Gully: a long, narrow ditch created by running water

Pewter: a metal made of tin mixed with lead or copper

Scholar: a person who has a great deal of knowledge in a particular field

Sinew: a band of tissue that connects a muscle to a bone

Tepee: a tent shaped like a cone and made from animal skins by North American Indians

Tendon: a strong, thick cord or band of tissue that joins a muscle to a bone or other body part

Terrain: an area of land

Places to Visit

Do you want to go on an expedition? Whether you visit online or in real life, re-create Sacagawea's journey for yourself.

Fort Mandan, North Dakota
fortmandan.com

Lewis and Clark National Historic Trail Interpretive Center, Great Falls, Montana
lewisandclarktrail.com/section3/ montanacities/greatfalls

Fort Clatsop National Monument, Oregon

nps.gov/lewi/planyourvisit/fortclatsop.htm

Pompey's Pillar National Monument, Montana

pompeyspillar.org

For more places to visit, go to:

nps.gov/nr/travel/lewisandclark/sitelist.htm

Bibliography

Exploring Lewis and Clark: Reflections on Men and Wilderness, Thomas P. Slaughter, Vintage Books, 2003.

Lewis & Clark: The Journey of the Corps of Discovery, Dayton Duncan and Ken Burns, Alfred A. Knopf, 1999.

On the Trail of Sacagawea, Peter Lourie, Boyds Mills Press, 2001.

Path to the Pacific: The Story of Sacagawea, Neta Lohnes Frazier, Sterling Publishing Company, 2007.

Sacagawea, Stacy DeKeyser, Scholastic, 2004.

Sacagawea: Crossing the Continent with Lewis & Clark, Emma Carlson Berne, Sterling Publishing Company, 2010.

Sacagawea: Guide for the Lewis and Clark Expedition, Hal Marcovitz, Chelsea House Publishers, 2001.

Sacagawea: Westward with Lewis and Clark, Alana J. White, Enslow Publishers, 1997.

Sacagawea's Son: The Life of Jean Baptiste Charbonneau, Marion Tinling, Mountain Press Publishing Company, 2001.

Index